The G

How to use this book:

This book is designed to be easy to follow and input your workouts into. Below is a quick overview of what the headers of the tables mean.

Term	Definition
Exercise	This is the movement you are performing.
Sets	This is how many groups of repetitions you perform.
Reps	This is how many times you bring the exercise through its range of motion before taking a break.
Weight	This is the amount of weight you are lifting.
RPE	This is a scale from 1-10 on how hard that exercise felt to you.
Rest	This is the time you take between sets.

RPE can be a valuable indicator to your progress, if you feel the RPE decreasing after a while, it may be time to increase the weight you are lifting.

There is also a notes section for anything that you feel you need to remind yourself of during the workout.

This book is designed to be simple to read, and use. There is enough room to accommodate even the most intense workouts.

\

Workout:_____ **Date:**_____

Exercise	Sets	Reps	Weight	RPE	Rest

Notes:

Workout:_____ **Date:**_____

Exercise	Sets	Reps	Weight	RPE	Rest

Notes:

Workout:_____ **Date:**_____

Exercise	Sets	Reps	Weight	RPE	Rest

Notes:

Workout:_____ **Date:**_____

Exercise	Sets	Reps	Weight	RPE	Rest

Notes:

Workout:_____ **Date:**_____

Exercise	Sets	Reps	Weight	RPE	Rest

Notes:

Workout:_____ **Date:**_____

Exercise	Sets	Reps	Weight	RPE	Rest

Notes:

Workout:_____ **Date:**_____

Exercise	Sets	Reps	Weight	RPE	Rest

Notes:

Workout:_____ **Date:**_____

Exercise	Sets	Reps	Weight	RPE	Rest

Notes:

Workout:_____ **Date:**_____

Exercise	Sets	Reps	Weight	RPE	Rest

Notes:

Workout:_____ **Date:**_____

Exercise	Sets	Reps	Weight	RPE	Rest

Notes:

Workout:_____ **Date:**_____

Exercise	Sets	Reps	Weight	RPE	Rest

Notes:

Workout:_____ **Date:**_____

Exercise	Sets	Reps	Weight	RPE	Rest

Notes:

Workout:_____ **Date:**_____

Exercise	Sets	Reps	Weight	RPE	Rest

Notes:

Workout:_____ **Date:**_____

Exercise	Sets	Reps	Weight	RPE	Rest

Notes:

Workout:_____ **Date:**_____

Exercise	Sets	Reps	Weight	RPE	Rest

Notes:

Workout:_____ **Date:**_____

Exercise	Sets	Reps	Weight	RPE	Rest

Notes:

Workout:_____ **Date:**_____

Exercise	Sets	Reps	Weight	RPE	Rest

Notes:

Workout:_____ **Date:**_____

Exercise	Sets	Reps	Weight	RPE	Rest

Notes:

Workout:_____ **Date:**_____

Exercise	Sets	Reps	Weight	RPE	Rest

Notes:

Workout:_____ **Date:**_____

Exercise	Sets	Reps	Weight	RPE	Rest

Notes:

Workout:_____ **Date:**_____

Exercise	Sets	Reps	Weight	RPE	Rest

Notes:

Workout:_____ **Date:**_____

Exercise	Sets	Reps	Weight	RPE	Rest

Notes:

Workout:_____ **Date:**_____

Exercise	Sets	Reps	Weight	RPE	Rest

Notes:

Workout:_____ **Date:**_____

Exercise	Sets	Reps	Weight	RPE	Rest

Notes:

Workout:_____ **Date:**_____

Exercise	Sets	Reps	Weight	RPE	Rest

Notes:

Workout:_____ **Date:**_____

Exercise	Sets	Reps	Weight	RPE	Rest

Notes:

Workout:_____ **Date:**_____

Exercise	Sets	Reps	Weight	RPE	Rest

Notes:

Workout:_____ Date:_____

Exercise	Sets	Reps	Weight	RPE	Rest

Notes:

Workout:_____ **Date:**_____

Exercise	Sets	Reps	Weight	RPE	Rest

Notes:

Workout:_____ **Date:**_____

Exercise	Sets	Reps	Weight	RPE	Rest

Notes:

Workout:_____   **Date:**_____

Exercise	Sets	Reps	Weight	RPE	Rest

Notes:

Workout:_____ **Date:**_____

Exercise	Sets	Reps	Weight	RPE	Rest

Notes:

Workout:_____ **Date:**_____

Exercise	Sets	Reps	Weight	RPE	Rest

Notes:

Workout:_____ **Date:**_____

Exercise	Sets	Reps	Weight	RPE	Rest

Notes:

Workout:_____ **Date:**_____

Exercise	Sets	Reps	Weight	RPE	Rest

Notes:

Workout:_____ **Date:**_____

Exercise	Sets	Reps	Weight	RPE	Rest

Notes:

Workout:_____ **Date:**_____

Exercise	Sets	Reps	Weight	RPE	Rest

Notes:

Workout:_____ **Date:**_____

Exercise	Sets	Reps	Weight	RPE	Rest

Notes:

Workout:_____ **Date:**_____

Exercise	Sets	Reps	Weight	RPE	Rest

Notes:

Workout:_____ **Date:**_____

Exercise	Sets	Reps	Weight	RPE	Rest

Notes:

Workout:_____ **Date:**_____

Exercise	Sets	Reps	Weight	RPE	Rest

Notes:

Workout:_____ **Date:**_____

Exercise	Sets	Reps	Weight	RPE	Rest

Notes:

Workout:_____ **Date:**_____

Exercise	Sets	Reps	Weight	RPE	Rest

Notes:

Workout:_____ **Date:**_____

Exercise	Sets	Reps	Weight	RPE	Rest

Notes:

Workout:_____ **Date:**_____

Exercise	Sets	Reps	Weight	RPE	Rest

Notes:

Workout:_____ **Date:**_____

Exercise	Sets	Reps	Weight	RPE	Rest

Notes:

Workout:_____ **Date:**_____

Exercise	Sets	Reps	Weight	RPE	Rest

Notes:

Workout:_____ **Date:**_____

Exercise	Sets	Reps	Weight	RPE	Rest

Notes:

Workout:_____ **Date:**_____

Exercise	Sets	Reps	Weight	RPE	Rest

Notes:

Workout:_____   Date:_____

Exercise	Sets	Reps	Weight	RPE	Rest

Notes:

Workout:_____ **Date:**_____

Exercise	Sets	Reps	Weight	RPE	Rest

Notes:

Workout:_____ **Date:**_____

Exercise	Sets	Reps	Weight	RPE	Rest

Notes:

Workout:_____ **Date:**_____

Exercise	Sets	Reps	Weight	RPE	Rest

Notes:

Workout:_____ **Date:**_____

Exercise	Sets	Reps	Weight	RPE	Rest

Notes:

Workout:_____ **Date:**_____

Exercise	Sets	Reps	Weight	RPE	Rest

Notes:

Workout:_____ **Date:**_____

Exercise	Sets	Reps	Weight	RPE	Rest

Notes:

Workout:_____ **Date:**_____

Exercise	Sets	Reps	Weight	RPE	Rest

Notes:

Workout:_____ **Date:**_____

Exercise	Sets	Reps	Weight	RPE	Rest

Notes:

Workout:_____ **Date:**_____

Exercise	Sets	Reps	Weight	RPE	Rest

Notes:

Workout:_____ **Date:**_____

Exercise	Sets	Reps	Weight	RPE	Rest

Notes:

Workout:_____ **Date:**_____

Exercise	Sets	Reps	Weight	RPE	Rest

Notes:

Workout:_____ **Date:**_____

Exercise	Sets	Reps	Weight	RPE	Rest

Notes:

Workout:_____ **Date:**_____

Exercise	Sets	Reps	Weight	RPE	Rest

Notes:

Workout:_____ **Date:**_____

Exercise	Sets	Reps	Weight	RPE	Rest

Notes:

Workout:_____ **Date:**_____

Exercise	Sets	Reps	Weight	RPE	Rest

Notes:

Workout:_____ **Date:**_____

Exercise	Sets	Reps	Weight	RPE	Rest

Notes:

Workout:_____ **Date:**_____

Exercise	Sets	Reps	Weight	RPE	Rest

Notes:

Workout:_____ **Date:**_____

Exercise	Sets	Reps	Weight	RPE	Rest

Notes:

Workout:_____ **Date:**_____

Exercise	Sets	Reps	Weight	RPE	Rest

Notes:

Workout:_____ **Date:**_____

Exercise	Sets	Reps	Weight	RPE	Rest

Notes:

Workout:_____ **Date:**_____

Exercise	Sets	Reps	Weight	RPE	Rest

Notes:

Workout:_____ **Date:**_____

Exercise	Sets	Reps	Weight	RPE	Rest

Notes:

Workout:_____ **Date:**_____

Exercise	Sets	Reps	Weight	RPE	Rest

Notes:

Workout:_____ **Date:**_____

Exercise	Sets	Reps	Weight	RPE	Rest

Notes:

Workout:_____ **Date:**_____

Exercise	Sets	Reps	Weight	RPE	Rest

Notes:

Workout:_____ **Date:**_____

Exercise	Sets	Reps	Weight	RPE	Rest

Notes:

Workout:_____ **Date:**_____

Exercise	Sets	Reps	Weight	RPE	Rest

Notes:

Workout:_____ **Date:**_____

Exercise	Sets	Reps	Weight	RPE	Rest

Notes:

Workout:_____ **Date:**_____

Exercise	Sets	Reps	Weight	RPE	Rest

Notes:

Workout:_____ **Date:**_____

Exercise	Sets	Reps	Weight	RPE	Rest

Notes:

Workout:_____ **Date:**_____

Exercise	Sets	Reps	Weight	RPE	Rest

Notes:

Workout:_____ **Date:**_____

Exercise	Sets	Reps	Weight	RPE	Rest

Notes:

Workout:_____ **Date:**_____

Exercise	Sets	Reps	Weight	RPE	Rest

Notes:

Workout:_____ **Date:**_____

Exercise	Sets	Reps	Weight	RPE	Rest

Notes:

Workout:_____ **Date:**_____

Exercise	Sets	Reps	Weight	RPE	Rest

Notes:

Workout:_____ **Date:**_____

Exercise	Sets	Reps	Weight	RPE	Rest

Notes:

Workout:_____ **Date:**_____

Exercise	Sets	Reps	Weight	RPE	Rest

Notes:

Workout:_____ **Date:**_____

Exercise	Sets	Reps	Weight	RPE	Rest

Notes:

Workout:_____ **Date:**_____

Exercise	Sets	Reps	Weight	RPE	Rest

Notes:

Workout:_____ **Date:**_____

Exercise	Sets	Reps	Weight	RPE	Rest

Notes:

Workout:_____ **Date:**_____

Exercise	Sets	Reps	Weight	RPE	Rest

Notes:

Workout:_____ **Date:**_____

Exercise	Sets	Reps	Weight	RPE	Rest

Notes:

Workout:_____ **Date:**_____

Exercise	Sets	Reps	Weight	RPE	Rest

Notes:

Workout:_____ **Date:**_____

Exercise	Sets	Reps	Weight	RPE	Rest

Notes:

Workout:_____ **Date:**_____

Exercise	Sets	Reps	Weight	RPE	Rest

Notes:

Workout:_____ **Date:**_____

Exercise	Sets	Reps	Weight	RPE	Rest

Notes:

Workout:_____ **Date:**_____

Exercise	Sets	Reps	Weight	RPE	Rest

Notes:

Workout:_____ **Date:**_____

Exercise	Sets	Reps	Weight	RPE	Rest

Notes:

Workout:_____ **Date:**_____

Exercise	Sets	Reps	Weight	RPE	Rest

Notes:

Workout:_____ **Date:**_____

Exercise	Sets	Reps	Weight	RPE	Rest

Notes:

Workout:_____ **Date:**_____

Exercise	Sets	Reps	Weight	RPE	Rest

Notes:

Workout:_____ **Date:**_____

Exercise	Sets	Reps	Weight	RPE	Rest

Notes:

Workout:_____ **Date:**_____

Exercise	Sets	Reps	Weight	RPE	Rest

Notes:

Workout:_____ **Date:**_____

Exercise	Sets	Reps	Weight	RPE	Rest

Notes:

Workout:_____ **Date:**_____

Exercise	Sets	Reps	Weight	RPE	Rest

Notes:

Workout:_____ **Date:**_____

Exercise	Sets	Reps	Weight	RPE	Rest

Notes:

Workout:_____ **Date:**_____

Exercise	Sets	Reps	Weight	RPE	Rest

Notes:

Workout:_____ **Date:**_____

Exercise	Sets	Reps	Weight	RPE	Rest

Notes:

About Me

I graduated from university with an honour's degree in science with a specialization in kinesiology, during my school I found a passion for trying to make fitness and exercise easy to digest so that everyone can reap the benefits of an active lifestyle.

This is the same workout tracking format I use, and it has helped me stay consistent, set achievable goals, and has reminded how far I have come on my fitness journey.

Made in the USA
Middletown, DE
22 July 2021